Networking Manual

Practical Strategies to Overcome Fear and Enhance Your Professional Relationships

© 2024 José María Sallés
© Design: José María Sallés
© Layaout: josemariasalles.com
Proofreadinmg and Translation: Anna Esteve

ISBN: 9798335482509

All rights reserved. No part of this work may be reproduced, stored in a retrieval system, or transmitted in any form or by any means (electronic, mechanical, photocopying, recording, or otherwise) without prior written permission from the copyright holders. Infringement of these rights may constitute a crime against intellectual property.

A Coffee Changes the Course

María had always believed that the key to success lay in hard work and determination, and while that was true, she would soon discover the real power of networking. With her small educational technology startup struggling to take off, every day felt like an uphill battle.

One rainy Wednesday, while working on her laptop from her usual corner in her favorite café, a familiar face greeted her with a smile. It was Sergi, a former university classmate and a well-known entrepreneur. After exchanging pleasantries and updating each other on their recent achievements, Sergi asked about her current project. María, somewhat hesitant but hopeful, shared her vision and the challenges she was facing.

Sergi listened attentively and then smiled, "María, I think I can help you." It turned out that Sergi had faced similar challenges and had overcome obstacles thanks to a formidable network of contacts he had cultivated over the years. "Networking isn't just about meeting people," Sergi said as he typed on his phone.

"It's about connecting with the right people, those who can open doors for you and offer new perspectives and opportunities".

Before the coffee had cooled, Sergi had already sent several emails introducing María to two investors and an expert in educational technology. Additionally, he invited her to a networking event the following week. "This is where real connections are forged," he asserted.

Inspired by the unexpected help, María attended the event. That night, surrounded by entrepreneurs and visionaries, she realized that each conversation was a seed of possibility. Talking with people who had been in her shoes, who had faced the same challenges and overcome them, was eye-opening. Each business card was a door to a new world of possibilities.

The following months were a whirlwind. With the support of the new contacts that Sergi had helped establish, and many more that she had cultivated since the event, María found not only investment but also valuable advice and strategic partnerships. Her startup began to gain traction, attracting interest from various parts of the country.

Looking back at the opening of her new office, María reflected on that casual meeting in the café. What had started as a rainy and gloomy day had turned into the catalyst for success she could never have imagined. She realized that networking was much more than a simple exchange of business cards; it was essential for the growth and development of not only her business but also her personal projects. In an interconnected world, isolation is the true enemy of progress.

.

Through the characters of María and Sergi, we see how networking, beyond simply meeting people, is crucial for discovering and seizing opportunities that might otherwise remain hidden. It demonstrates how human connections can radically transform the fate of a business or project, opening up a range of possibilities that surpass what can be achieved by working alone.

Are you maximizing the networking opportunities available to you?

Consider the possibility of having coffee with someone new or attending that next event. You never know what doors might open with a simple conversation.

As you explore this manual, you will discover key strategies that will equip you to make networking a powerful tool in your professional and personal development. This booklet unveils all the secrets to mastering the art of networking. It is a comprehensive guide designed to help you build powerful relationships and achieve the success you seek.

"The Beautiful ART of Dealing with People in Business"

... We've always done it, even if we didn't call it NETWORKING

Foreword

Networking undoubtedly stands as a vital tool for the advancement of our projects, both professionally and personally.

Relationships play a crucial role as key resources to achieve various objectives, from obtaining information to securing an advantageous position in a specific environment. These interactions mostly unfold naturally.

Although I'm not unveiling any extraordinary revelation, my purpose with this booklet is to provide you with a review of knowledge I've gathered over time. While familiar, sometimes these concepts need to be revisited. The importance of this action lies in consolidating concepts we already possess.

This is not a book to read cover to cover; it's a reference manual. So, open the booklet to any page you prefer and revisit those concepts you likely already know. At some point, they will lead you to valuable reflection.

Table of Contents

1. What is Networking?
    - Contribution of Networking in Business
2. How to Build an Effective Network
3. Theory of Six Degrees of Separation
4. Where and How to Network?
    - How to Network? Preliminary Phase "PRE"
    - How to Network? Interactive Phase "IN"
    - How to Network? Post Phase "POST"
5. Preparing Your "Elevator Pitch"
6. Overcoming the "Fear" and Embarrassment of Networking
    - Please People!
    - Convince People!
7. The Main Key to Success in Networking
    - Personal Keys to Success in Projects
8. WCONNECTA
9. Networking in Action

"Networking is a Key Element for COLLABORATION"

> *In contrast to other species, sapiens have the unique ability to collaborate exceptionally flexibly with a large number of unknown individuals beyond the limits of their social group. This skill has been fundamental to their dominance in the world.*
>
> - Yuval Noah Harari - Sapiens

1
What is Networking?

Contribution of Networking to Business

What is Networking?

Networking is a skill that facilitates the creation, expansion, and maintenance of a network of contacts and professional relationships.

This talent not only involves establishing initial connections but also the ability to maintain these relationships over time, generating continuous benefits throughout your professional career. In an increasingly competitive business world, your success depends more than ever on how well you manage your relationships.

Networking presents itself as a strategic tool that goes beyond merely expanding contacts. It is a fundamental investment in your professional growth.

While many people may naturally find it easy to build professional relationships, networking is a skill that can be learned and improved.

Contribution of Networking to Business

The key contributions of networking in business include:

1 CREATION OF OPPORTUNITIES.
Expansion of Connections

Networking expands your circle of contacts, giving you access to a diversity of people and professions.

The more connections you have, the greater the chances of discovering job opportunities, collaborative projects, or even new clients.

2 PROFESSIONAL DEVELOPMENT.
Mentorship and Advice

Through networking, you will establish relationships with more experienced professionals who have different knowledge and can become your mentors.

Take advantage of these mentors who can offer valuable guidance, sharing their experiences and knowledge to help drive your professional development.

3. ACCESS TO RESOURCES AND INFORMATION
Information Flow

Maintaining an active network keeps you up-to-date with the latest trends, market opportunities, and industry changes.

Your connections will provide you with valuable information that can make a difference in your decision-making and professional strategies.

4 BUSINESS GROWTH.
Collaborations and Partnerships

In the business world, networking is essential for establishing strategic collaborations and partnerships.

Building strong relationships with other entrepreneurs or professionals in the sector is fundamental for the growth and expansion of your company.

5 CONTINUOUS LEARNING OPPORTUNITIES.
Knowledge Exchange

Networking is not only about what you can gain but also about what you can offer. It's a win-win relationship.

Sharing your knowledge and experiences with others not only reinforces your position as a professional but also gives you the opportunity to learn from the perspectives, viewpoints, and experiences of others.

6 ADAPTATION TO CHANGE.
Professional Flexibility

In a constantly changing work environment, a good network of contacts acts as a lifeline. Connecting with people who have gone through similar transitions or who have complementary skills facilitates adaptation to new circumstances and professional challenges.

7 VISIBILITY AND PERSONAL BRANDING.
Building a Personal Brand

Strong connections in the professional realm contribute to building your personal brand. Being known and respected in your network increases your visibility and reputation, which in turn generates opportunities and trust in your knowledge and skills.

8. INFLUENCE AND PERSUASION.
Building Lasting Relationships

Effective networking is based on building authentic and lasting relationships. These strong connections not only open doors but also allow you to exert influence ethically.

The trust developed over time is a key element when seeking support from your colleagues or leading teams.

Contribution of Networking to Business

- Creation of Opportunities
- Professional Development
- Access to Resources and Information
- Business Growth
- Continuous Learning
- Adaptation to Change
- Visibility and Personal Branding
- Influence and Persuasion

Contribution of Networking to Business

SOME FACTS ABOUT THE EFFECTIVENESS OF NETWORKING

<u>Generation of Business Opportunities:</u>
According to a HubSpot survey, 85% of professionals and executives believe they have established closer and more meaningful relctionships with other companies through networking.

<u>Increase in Job Opportunities:</u>
LinkedIn has reported that 70% of people worldwide have been hired at companies where they have a connection, either direct or indirect, highlighting the importance of professional networks.

<u>Increase in Knowledge and Perspectives:</u>
A Forbes report indicates that 78% of professionals consider networking crucial for their career development, allowing them to gain new perspectives and knowledge.

Contribution of Networking to Business

AUTHOR'S NOTES ...

Recently, I had the privilege of conversing with a distinguished professor from one of the most prestigious business schools in Spain about the evolution of networking in the business world. Our discussion focused on the changing perception of this practice over the years.

The professor shared with me his perspective on how, not too long ago, networking was not well-regarded in certain business and educational circles. He recalled a time when the term "salespeople" was used pejoratively, associated with a negative image of people seeking business opportunities at any cost.

However, as the professor highlighted, we have experienced a radical shift in this mentality. Nowadays, networking is recognized as a fundamental tool for business success. It is no longer simply about selling but about establishing strong and lasting relationships that generate mutual opportunities and business growth.

2

How to Build an Effective Network of Contacts

How to Build an Effective Network of Contacts

In today's world, building an effective network of contacts is essential. Every connection established is a bridge to professional opportunities and personal growth.

In this chapter, we will lay the foundations for cultivating strong and effective relationships that can drive our success in the professional realm and beyond.

Imagine your network of contacts as a web of bridges connecting you to different aspects of the professional and business world. The higher the quality, robustness, and effectiveness of your network, the easier it will be to navigate professional challenges and seize opportunities. Building this network involves cultivating genuine and meaningful relationships. Every interaction is an opportunity to establish beneficial long-term connections.

> "Given the way the business world is changing, smart networking (making contacts and building relationships) is more important than ever before."
> - Wayne E. Baker, MBA University of Chicago -

The planning of strategies to identify and connect with key contacts involves two steps:

1. Identification of Key Contacts:

Definition of Objectives:
Before you start building your network, it is crucial to have clarity about your goals. Define what type of contacts are key to your sector or professional objectives. Ask yourself who the individuals or groups are whose influence or knowledge can benefit you professionally.

Research and Segmentation:
Conduct research to identify key people in your field. Use online platforms, attend professional events, and stay updated on thought leaders in your sector.

Segment your potential contacts according to their relevance to your goals.

2. Establishment of Authentic and Lasting Relationships:

Focus on Authenticity and Ethics:
When building your network, prioritize authenticity over excessive self-promotion. Share your experiences, interests, and goals genuinely. Authenticity and ethics build trust, which is fundamental for lasting relationships.

Long-Term Relationships:
Effective networking is not just about making superficial connections; it's about building long-term relationships. Cultivate these relationships by investing time in understanding the needs and challenges of your contacts, and look for ways to be helpful to them.

How to Build an Effective Network of Contacts

AUTHOR'S NOTES ...

The Law of Gravity in Effective Networking

In the vast universe of professional relationships, effective networking follows the invisible law of gravity: from top to bottom. Just as celestial bodies move towards the force exerted by the Earth, in the business realm, the most fruitful connections are established when connecting with those who hold decision-making power.

It is preferable to direct our efforts towards the top of the corporate pyramid, where CEOs and executive leaders are found, as they possess the power to influence strategic and high-level decisions.

Connecting with decision-makers in the company not only opens doors to unique opportunities but also ensures that information and relationships flow organically downwards to middle management and employees. Just as planets orbit around the sun, communications and actions within a company tend to gravitate towards the direction set by its leaders.

How to Build an Effective Network of Contacts

The right connections can be the key to unlocking success.

An experience I had demonstrated the effectiveness of the "Law of Gravity in Networking." Such was the case with an innovative project we promoted in collaboration with a major telecommunications company in the country. The contacts started from the bottom up: account executive, zone director, and regional director. Everything seemed to be going smoothly until the project reached a critical point, where the regional interests of the regional director threatened to overshadow the national benefits. The situation became tense, and the project reached a deadlock, desperately needing a push to move beyond the regional limits.

It was at this crucial moment that the true magic of networking became evident. In a meeting with an executive from a financial entity, using the skill of connecting seemingly unrelated ideas, I managed to establish direct contact with the president of the telecommunications company, bringing the project to his attention and showing him its potential on a national level.

The response was immediate and transformative. The president issued orders to the regional director, ensuring alignment of objectives at all levels of the company.

From that moment on, the project took off, driven by a shared vision and renewed commitment to its full scope and potential. I still remember the look the regional director gave me at our first meeting after receiving the president's instructions; the saying "if looks could kill" came to mind.

This story highlights a crucial principle in the business world: the importance of establishing direct connections with decision-makers. Reaching out to those who have the power to decide can completely transform the trajectory of a project or negotiation. It is essential, whenever possible, to reach and persuade these key figures, as they are the ones who ultimately have the capacity to move resources, change policies, and give the green light to new initiatives. Understanding and practicing this approach can mean the difference between stagnation and significant progress in a project.

3
Theory of Six Degrees of Separation

"It's a small world"

Theory of Six Degrees of Separation

According to Frigyes Karinthy, any person can be connected to any other person on the planet through a chain of acquaintances that has no more than five intermediaries, linking both individuals with just six links.

The concept is based on the idea that the number of acquaintances grows exponentially with the number of contacts or relationships in the chain, and only a small number of connections are necessary for the entire human population to be within reach.

Although the theory of six degrees is not a rigid rule and can vary according to cultural and regional contexts, it remains an intriguing concept that highlights the surprising interconnectedness of human society.

***Frigyes Karinthy** (Budapest, June 24, 1887 — Siófok, August 29, 1938).
A Hungarian writer, he was the first to propose the theory of six degrees of separation, originating from his 1929 short story "Chains."

Theory of Six Degrees of Separation

The notion that we are all closer than we imagine underscores the importance of networking and interpersonal connections in an increasingly interconnected world.

Imagine for a moment your global network of contacts as an intricate web of interpersonal connections that stretches across the world. At the heart of this network is your "first-level zone," which encompasses your direct contacts: friends, colleagues, and acquaintances with whom you interact regularly. However, the true magnitude of your network is revealed when we explore your "second-level zone." This area includes the contacts of your direct contacts, that is, your indirect contacts, creating an expanded network of potential connections. These are the "bridges" that link you to other circles and consequently to new opportunities.

Now, consider this scenario: in Spain, we have an average of 536* first-level contacts. This implies that, just through one person, your direct contacts, you could have access to over 280,000 contacts!

According to a study by the Social Observatory of 'La Caixa', the average Spaniard knows 536 people directly.

Theory of Six Degrees of Separation

This astonishing figure illustrates the power and reach of our connections in the modern era.

Cultivating and nurturing these relationships not only expands our opportunities but also enriches our lives with new perspectives and experiences. So the next time you find yourself meeting a new contact, remember the potential that lies within each connection. Make the most of your network, both at the first level and the second, and discover the infinite possibilities that unfold before you.

Vital!

In efficient networking, responsibility and ethics are fundamental pillars. By using our personal networks responsibly and ethically, we not only strengthen our connections and professional opportunities but also contribute to a more ethical and trustworthy business environment for everyone.

Theory of Six Degrees of Separation

AUTHOR'S NOTES ...

As we have seen, the theory of six degrees of separation suggests that anyone on the planet can be connected to any other person through a chain of acquaintances that has no more than five intermediaries.

To illustrate how you could be connected, for example, to the "Pope in Rome" through only six degrees or less, here is an example:

1. *You - Start with yourself.*
2. *A friend of yours - You have a friend who is very active in community activities and attends international events.*
3. *A clergyman known by your friend - This friend knows a clergyman who has worked on international Church projects and frequently travels to conferences abroad.*
4. *A bishop - The clergyman personally knows several bishops and cardinals due to his work in the Church.*
5. *A cardinal - One of these bishops is close to a cardinal who is part of the Vatican's inner circle.*
6. *The Pope in Rome - The cardinal has direct access to the Pope and meets with him regularly to discuss Church matters.*

Theory of Six Degrees of Separation

Or if you prefer, you can connect with Formula 1 driver Fernando Alonso:

1. *You - Start with yourself, interested in connecting with Fernando Alonso.*
2. *A motorsport enthusiast friend - You have a friend who is a big fan of car racing and frequently attends motorsport events.*
3. *Racing event organizer - This friend personally knows a racing event organizer who frequently interacts with drivers and teams in international competitions.*
4. *Member of a Formula 1 team - The organizer has connections with several members of Formula 1 teams, including engineers and managers who work directly with the drivers.*
5. *Formula 1 team manager - One of these team members is close to the manager of a team where Fernando Alonso has raced or currently collaborates.*
6. *Fernando Alonso - The manager has direct and frequent contact with Fernando Alonso, both at races and related events.*

Theory of Six Degrees of Separation

These examples demonstrate how, through a chain of connections starting from your own social circles and extending through professional and leisure relationships, it is theoretically possible to connect with a public figure like the Pope of Rome or Fernando Alonso. This model underscores the interconnectedness and potential of social networks to bridge the gap between people from various fields.

Author's Video on
Frigyes Karinthy's Six
Degrees of Separation
Theory

4
Where and How to Network?

Where and How to Network?

Networking, understood as the creation of professional contact networks, is a versatile activity that is not limited to a specific time or place. Whether at formal events, casual meetings, conferences, chance encounters, or even in the digital world, each situation presents unique opportunities to forge valuable professional connections.

Different scenarios that provide the perfect opportunity for networking:

1. Professional Social Networks
Networking has become an indispensable activity in the work world. For this reason, digital tools that promote the formation of professional relationships quickly and effectively are continuously developed. These platforms facilitate the creation of work networks that serve as job markets, databases of potential clients, and resources for finding investors or business partners.
It is essential that your profile is complete and updated with relevant information, as well as a professional photo and a compelling summary.

Where and How to Network?

It is recommended to join groups related to your sector to participate in discussions and expand your reach.

2. Events, Conferences, and Fairs
Attend both virtual and in-person events to create and leverage networking opportunities face-to-face.

3. Online Forums and Communities
Get involved in online forums and communities related to your industry. Contribute to conversations and questions, demonstrating that you are an active professional in your field.

4. Unexpected Encounters
In these situations, being adaptable, flexible, and ready to seize any opportunity that arises is crucial. It's important to relate topics to steer the conversation towards your interests. In these cases, the "elevator pitch" becomes extremely important.
Networking is much more than just a social interaction or exchanging business cards at events.
It is a powerful tool that drives professional growth and opens doors to new opportunities. To make the most of its potential, it is essential to understand and master the effective strategies that support it

Where and How to Network?

It develops over a continuous process that spans three stages. These stages include a preparation phase, a moment of direct interaction, and follow-up after the established connections.

1. Preliminary Phase ("PRE"):
The preparation phase is crucial. It involves researching the attendees, defining clear objectives, and having a well-crafted strategy. This stage before the event lays the foundation for effective participation and maximizes opportunities for effective connections.

2. Interactive Phase ("IN"):
During the event, we enter the interaction phase, the central moment where connections are made. It's the time to apply the prior preparation, present ourselves impactfully, and actively engage in meaningful conversations. This phase requires agility, authenticity, and readiness for building valuable relationships.

3. Follow-up Phase ("POST")
Here, the focus is on nurturing and consolidating the established relationships. This stage is essential to keep the network alive and open doors to future opportunities.

Where and How to Network?

These three phases, each playing a unique role, form an integral process that maximizes the value of planned networking, from preparation to relationship consolidation.

Networking is not hunting;
it is farming

Where and How to Network?

AUTHOR'S NOTES ...

Opportunities to make meaningful connections are everywhere, even in the most unexpected places. Networking can happen at any time and place, and being prepared to capitalize on those opportunities can make a difference in your career and life.

Imagine this: you are in line at the supermarket, patiently waiting your turn to pay. You strike up a conversation with the person behind you. It turns out they are a professional in your same field, and after a few minutes of casual chat, you exchange business cards. That brief interaction at the grocery store could lead to a valuable professional connection you never expected to find in that place.

Or consider this situation: you are walking your dog in a local park when you meet another person who is also with their pet. While the dogs play energetically together, you strike up a casual conversation with the other dog owner. You discover that you share similar professional interests. As the chat flows, you exchange ideas and experiences and as you say goodbye, you realize that this casual conversation in the park could open doors you never imagined.

Where and How to Network?

From formal events to casual encounters in everyday life, as we mentioned at the beginning of the chapter, networking can happen at any time and place. The important thing is to be open to new opportunities, maintain a receptive attitude, and be prepared to capitalize on those connections when they arise.

The ability to relate topics reveals itself as an invaluable asset in networking. The capacity to find connections between seemingly disparate concepts creates opportunities and opens new doors to innovation and problem-solving.
Mastering this skill allows building bridges between ideas, fostering interdisciplinary collaboration and generating unique solutions.

"The power of networking lies in our willingness to capitalize on every encounter, transforming simple conversations into professional opportunities."

Preliminary Phase "PRE"

As a professional, entrepreneur, or business owner, it is imperative to attend professional events, conferences, and seminars related to your sector. This strategic participation is not just an opportunity but a responsibility to drive the growth of your business or to find strategic options for your project.

In this regard, prior preparation becomes essential. It is important to dedicate time to researching the participants and companies, understanding the event's objectives, and preparing your "elevator pitch" that highlights your strengths. This advanced preparation not only maximizes the effectiveness of your interactions but also helps you stand out and make the most of the opportunities the event offers.

Where and How to Network? Preliminary Phase "PRE"

How Should We Plan Events?

1. Research Process:
Before a networking event, preparation is key. In-depth research on participants, companies, and the event's dynamics creates a foundation for valuable connections and opportunities. With this strategic knowledge, identifying key contacts is streamlined, and more effective conversations with contacts are facilitated.

Having extensive information about our interlocutor provides a significant advantage in negotiations by allowing us to build trust, tailor our approach, identify points of agreement, handle objections, and create strong relationships. This increases our chances of success and positions us favorably to achieve our business objectives.

2. Setting Objectives:
When planning the event, it is essential to establish clear objectives that will help you make the most of the experience. Here are some examples of objectives you might consider:

Meet New People
Set a quantitative goal, such as meeting at least five new contacts.

Relevant Contacts
Define what type of contacts you want to establish.

Deepen Existing Relationships
If you already have contacts attending the event, you might set a goal to strengthen those relationships by scheduling a more extended meeting.

Seek Collaboration Opportunities
Set a specific goal to explore potential collaborations or strategic partnerships with other companies or professionals.

3. Prepare Your Elevator Pitch:
The "Elevator Pitch" is very useful in situations where you need to introduce yourself quickly and concisely. Preparing it will serve as a valuable exercise in reflection. Develop a brief and compelling speech that highlights who you are and what you do, aiming to deliver this in the time it would take for a short elevator ride, between 30 seconds and 2 minutes

Video from the Author
with a Personal Experience
on the Preliminary Phase
(PRE) of Networking

*A special chapter on the "Elevator Pitch" will be developed later.

Networking: Preliminary Phase "PRE"

1. Research Process

2. Setting Objectives

3. Preparing Your Quick Presentation, the so-called "Elevator Pitch"

Interactive Phase "IN"

Maximizing networking opportunities at events and effective techniques for establishing connections with new people.

1. Be Proactive and Authentic
Being proactive in interactions means taking the initiative to guide the conversation effectively. Be yourself and show authenticity in the conversation. Sincerity creates a solid foundation for building genuine relationships.

2. Develop a Positive and Open Attitude
Display a positive and open attitude. The first impression is crucial, and a positive attitude creates a conducive environment for an effective connection.

3. Maintain Open Body Language:
Body language is fundamental in social interactions. Maintain an open posture, make eye contact, and smile to convey confidence and openness.

4. Start the Conversation with a Friendly Greeting
Begin the interaction with a warm and friendly greeting. A simple "hello" followed by your name creates a starting point for the conversation

5. Use Open-Ended Questions
Ask open-ended questions that encourage more detailed responses. This not only shows interest in the other person but also provides opportunities to develop the conversation. Remember that open-ended questions start with "why," "how," or "what."

6. Active Listening
Focus on what the other person is communicating. Active listening is essential to understand their ideas, demonstrate empathy, and forge a more meaningful connection.

7. Find Common Ground and Relate Concepts
Identify shared interests or experiences that can serve as common ground. This helps to establish a shared space and offers meaningful topics for dialogue. Use the ability to relate and find connections between seemingly disparate concepts.

8. Use the Person's Name
Use the person's name during the conversation. This personalizes the interaction and shows interest in remembering important details.

9. Two People. Avoid Interruption
In a conversation, there are two interlocutors. Avoid interrupting the other person while they are speaking. Let them express their ideas before sharing yours. This demonstrates respect and attention.

10. Be Aware of Non-Verbal Cues
Observe the other person's non-verbal signals to gauge their level of comfort. If they seem receptive, continue the conversation naturally. If they show signs of discomfort, be respectful and consider adjusting your approach.

11. The Relationship Should Always Be Win-Win
During the conversation, look for ways to offer help or value. Ask about their challenges and consider how you can contribute positively to their goals.

12. Exchange Contact Information
If the conversation is going well and you see a basis for future interactions, exchange contact information naturally. This facilitates follow-up and the building of the relationship.

13. Use the Elevator Pitch
Have a brief speech prepared that highlights who you are and what you do. This can be useful in situations where you need to introduce yourself quickly and concisely.

14. Share Brief Personal Stories
If time permits, you can share brief anecdotes or personal stories. This humanizes the interaction and allows the other person to get to know you more authentically.

Where and How to Network? Interactive Phase "IN"

AUTHOR'S NOTES...

The Art of Relating: My Promotional Experience as a Writer

When I published my first book, "El Camionero Recomienda," in 2006 and embarked on a promotional tour on radio and television, I had a clear focus in mind: to relate every topic of conversation to my company, Wtransnet. From questions about the secrets behind my book to challenges in Spanish cuisine, I always found a way to link the conversation back to Wtransnet.

When asked about the genesis of the idea behind a book dedicated to roadside restaurants, I always found an opportunity to highlight the fundamental role of Wtransnet in the evolution of freight transport in Europe. Seizing the context, I would mention how this platform has gone beyond being a simple load and truck exchange to become a vital connection point for thousands of transporters traveling European roads daily. This strategic narrative not only contributed to increased book sales but also cemented Wtransnet's position as a key player in the transportation industry at the national level.

Where and How to Network? Interactive Phase "IN"

Every interview was an opportunity to demonstrate the power of relating seemingly disparate concepts, thereby sharing the success story behind Wtransnet.

Networking: Interactive Phase "IN"

1. Proactive and Authentic
2. Positive and Open Attitude
3. SMILE, Open Body Language
4. Friendly Greeting
5. Open-Ended Questions
6. Active Listening
7. Find Common Ground and Relate Concepts
8. Use the Person's Name
9. Two People. No Interruption
10. Attentive to Non-Verbal Cues
11. Win-Win Relationship
12. Exchange Contact Information
13. Use "Elevator Pitch"
14. Share Brief Personal Stories

A smile is an essential element in interpersonal relationships; it acts as a key that opens doors.

"The man whose face does not smile should not open a shop."

-Chinese Proverb-

Post-Event Phase "POST"

In the "POST" phase, follow-up is essential for effectively maintaining long-term relationships.

Tips

1. Continuous Interaction
Maintain regular communication with your contacts. Whether through emails, phone calls, social media messages, or in-person meetings, consistency in communication is key to keeping the relationship alive.

2. Personal Reminders
Make an effort or use your planner to remember personal details about your contacts, such as birthdays, anniversaries, or significant events in their lives. Sending a personalized message on special occasions shows that you value the relationship beyond the professional level.

3. Offering Help and Support
Keep an eye on the needs and challenges of your contacts. Provide your help and support proactively. Ask how you can be beneficial to them.

4. Common Interests
Identify and nurture shared interests. Whether in the professional or personal realm, finding common ground will strengthen the connection. These could be collaborative projects, hobbies, or even events that both of you are interested in attending.

5. Regular Updates:
Keeping your contacts updated on your professional journey has several advantages. It not only keeps them informed about your current achievements and challenges but can also open doors to new opportunities. Additionally, by keeping your contacts informed, you can strengthen your relationships and maintain a strong and active support network.

6 Face-to-Face Meetings: Whenever possible, organize or join face-to-face meetings. Nothing replaces the authenticity of an in-person interaction or a handshake. These meetings can be lunches, coffees, or even professional events where both of you can attend.

7. Be Proactive in the Connection
Don't always wait for the other person to initiate the connection. Be proactive in sending

messages, sharing relevant news, or proposing meetings. Taking the initiative shows genuine interest in maintaining the relationship.

8. Show Gratitude
Express gratitude for the relationship and for your contacts' contributions over time. A simple thank you can strengthen the bond and create an atmosphere of mutual appreciation.

9. Be Authentic
Long-term relationships are built on trust, and authenticity helps in building that trust.

10. Adapt to Changes
Professional and personal life is constantly changing. Be flexible and adaptable as circumstances evolve. Adjust the dynamics of the relationship as necessary to accommodate new responsibilities, locations, or priorities.

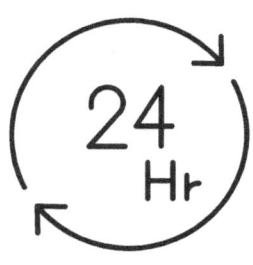

It's important to note that following up within 24 to 48 hours after a meeting is an essential practice, not just in sales but also in cultivating strong professional relationships.

This not only demonstrates courtesy and professionalism but also reinforces the initial impression, clarifies any potential questions or concerns, and maintains the momentum of the conversation.

Networking: Post-Event Phase "POST"

1. Continuous Interaction
2. Personal Reminders
3. Offering Help and Support
4. Common Interests
5. Regular Updates
6. Face-to-Face Meetings
7. Be Proactive in the Connection
8. Show Gratitude
9. Be Authentic
10. Adapt to Changes

Where and How to Network? Post-Event Phase "POST"

NOTAS DEL AUTOR ...

"The key to success in networking interviews is to keep an open and unbiased mind."

At the end of the first WCONNECTA, the event we promised would be a milestone in business networking for road freight transport, I wanted to find out if we had delivered on our promise. I approached the attendees, seeking stories of success, fruitful contacts, and possible closed deals. Among the multitude of enthusiastic responses, one in particular resonated with unexpected depth.

One of the participants, with a gleam of surprise in his eyes, shared with me his peculiar victory. "It went very well for me! I made five very good contacts and one excellent one," he said, making a distinction that piqued my curiosity. I asked him, "What is the difference between a good contact and an excellent one?" The answer was filled with a touching simplicity and profound meaning. "Excellent," he explained, "because it was with someone from my own town, a former competitor with whom I hadn't spoken for years. We are competitors, and our relationship was, until now, non-existent."

"It's ironic to attend an event far from our town and discover that the most valuable contact was so close to home."

In an unexpected conversation, when they found themselves face-to-face, they considered collaboration possibilities they had never thought of before. "You have a yard, a large parking area for trucks," he suggested to his new/old acquaintance. Together, they imagined and agreed to share this space, reducing costs and doubling benefits—a clever solution to an old problem.

This anecdote illustrates a fundamental truth about human and professional relationships: often, prejudices and prior expectations cloud our judgment, closing doors that could open up unforeseen horizons. By attending WCONNECTA, both businessmen brought more than just business cards; they also carried the burden of a past conflict that, when reconsidered under a new light, transformed into a promising alliance.

Thus, the first WCONNECTA not only achieved its goal of bringing professionals together under one roof but also demonstrated that the true success of a meeting can lie in the most unexpected connections.

It reminded us of the importance of approaching each dialogue with an open mind, ready to rediscover and reinvent, even when the setting and the people seem familiar.

5

Prepare Your "ELEVATOR PITCH"

The "elevator pitch" is a brief and direct presentation that summarizes who you are, what you do, and your objectives. It should capture the listener's interest, all in the time it takes for a short elevator ride.

This pitch should clearly demonstrate your value and why they should be interested in you.

Prepare Your Presentation: "ELEVATOR PITCH"

When you're in a position to interact with your contacts, you'll need to present your project, business proposal, or professional aspirations. Often, you must do this concisely, similar to the duration of a brief elevator ride. Your goal is to capture your listener's interest to get an opportunity to present your proposal in more detail and without haste.

How should you prepare a professional "elevator pitch"?

First, let's go over the basics:

1. Briefly Define Your Services or Products
Concisely define what you do, your role, and the name of your company, if applicable.

2. Highlight the Most Important Value
Focus on the value you bring and the advantages of your services or products.

What makes you different? What advantages do you have over your competition?

"Elevator Pitch"

3. Tangible Achievements
Add credibility to your pitch with tangible achievements or concrete examples.

4. Tell a Brief "Story"
Narrative elements have the power to emotionally connect with your listener. If time allows, share a brief personal "story."

Let's see how the message should be:

5. Be Concise
Express your ideas or information clearly and directly.

6. Simple and Clear Language
Use simple and clear language. Avoid jargon.

The ending of your message is very important.

7. End Positively with a "Call to Action"
At the end, say goodbye with a positive attitude, showing interest in maintaining communication or suggesting future meetings.

t's important to include a <u>call to action</u> or propose the next step yourself. Always try to

"Elevator Pitch"

keep the initiative, or as the saying goes, "keep the ball in your court."

One of the secrets to making an effective "elevator pitch" is...

8. Practice, Practice, Practice
Practice your tone and pace to make your presentation more engaging and captivating. This will help you overcome nerves and convey confidence.

Keep in mind that "What you say is just as important as how you say it."

9. Be Authentic
Authenticity creates a stronger connection with your listener.

10. Add Passion!
Season your pitch with a pinch of "passion." Your enthusiasm and passion create positive energy that is contagious.

11. Adapt It!

Tailor your presentation to your listener and their interests, and update it with your latest achievements and goals.

Remember: The goal of the "elevator pitch" is not to deliver all the information possible, but to capture interest and generate a more extensive conversation.

"Elevator Pitch"
___

AUTHOR'S NOTES ...

To illustrate how an effective 'elevator pitch' can capture an investor's interest and open doors for future conversations, I present the following example. In it, we can analyze how the key elements of a persuasive speech are articulated in a brief but crucial encounter.

<u>Context:</u>
During a health technology conference, Sandra, the founder of "HealthTrack," meets Marc, an investor known for his focus on sustainable innovations in the health sector.

<u>The Elevator Encounter:</u>
Sandra: *Hi, Marc. I'm Sandra from HealthTrack.*

① *We transform personal health management with an app that uses AI to provide real-time personalized health recommendations.*

② *Our system is not only intuitive but also anticipates health needs, preventing major issues.*

1. *Briefly define your product and services*
2. *Highlight the most important value*

"Elevator Pitch"
___

Marc: *How interesting.*

Sandra: *Unlike many, our app integrates behavioral data with medical histories to offer proactive predictions and advice. This has resulted in a 40% reduction in emergency room visits among our users, demonstrating our direct impact on people's lives and on reducing medical costs.*
.

Marc: *That's impressive. How did it all start?*

Sandra: *It all began when my grandfather suffered a health complication that could have been prevented. I realized that many apps react but don't prevent. So, with my team, we decided to change that.*

Marc: *Wow, it's really personal for you.*

3. *Highlight the most important value - Differentiate from the competition. Tangible achievements.*
4. *Brief story - emotional touch.*

"Elevator Pitch"
___

Sandra: Yes, every feature of our app aims to make users feel not just attended to, but genuinely cared for. We're looking for partners to help us bring this technology to more people worldwide.

⑤

Would you be interested in exploring how we can collaborate on this effort?

Marc: Definitely, let's talk more after we get out of here.

⑥

Sandra: Perfect, Marc. I'll call you tomorrow to arrange a meeting. Thank you for your time!

5. Positive farewell with a call to action.
6. Keeping the initiative on your side.

This "elevator pitch" includes a brief personal story that adds an emotional and authentic touch, highlighting HealthTrack's unique value and setting it apart from the competition. Sandra also uses simple and clear language, avoiding jargon, making it easy for Marc to understand and become interested. Additionally, her positive and proactive attitude at the end shows her interest in maintaining communication and taking the initiative for the next step.

Think ...

Brief description of your services or products, "what you do"

Your most important values / What sets you apart, what makes you special?

Think ...

Tangible achievements

Notes

Notes

"Elevator Pitch"

AUTHORS'S NOTES ...

Imagine a vibrant scene in a bustling skyscraper, where elevators are more than just vertical transport—they are stages for brilliant displays of persuasion and wit: the "elevator pitches."

In these brief moments of encounter, where brevity is essential and impressions are crucial, professionals and entrepreneurs become masters of conciseness and persuasion. But did you know that the concept of the "elevator pitch" has its roots in Hollywood? It is said that the expression originated in the 1930s and 40s when screenwriters tried to sell their movie ideas to studio executives during brief elevator encounters.

Yet, the "elevator pitch" is not just for the world of cinema. In Silicon Valley, startups compete for investors' attention in their building lobbies, while at business conferences around the globe, professionals strive to catch the interest of potential collaborators in crowded hallways.

One of the most fascinating anecdotes about the "elevator pitch" involves a young entrepreneur named Brian Chesky. In 2008, while seeking funding for his fledgling startup Airbnb, he

"Elevator Pitch"

approached a major investor in an elevator. In just a few seconds, Chesky managed to capture the investor's attention and secured a meeting that eventually led to a crucial investment for his company's success.

But the "elevator pitch" isn't limited to big corporations and renowned startups. From university students to freelance professionals, everyone can benefit from mastering this skill.

In the modern world, where time is a precious resource and opportunities can arise at any moment, the "elevator pitch" has become an indispensable tool for standing out in a sea of competition. Like a magician with words, every word counts, and every elevator encounter is an opportunity to create magic.

Think and prepare your elevator pitch well—you might need it at any moment.

How to Prepare Your "Elevator Pitch"

1. Define Your Services/Products - What Do You Do?
2. Highlight Your Most Important Value
3. Tangible Achievements
4. Tell a Brief Story
5. Be Concise
6. Use Simple and Clear Language
7. End Positively with a Call to Action
8. Practice, Practice, Practice
9. Be Authentic
10. Show Passion
11. Continuously Adapt to Your Listener and the Time Available

Video of the author with experiences from the chapter "Elevator Pitch"

6

Overcoming Fear and Embarrassment in Networking

Make People Like You

Convince People!

Overcoming the Fear and Embarrassment of Networking

The fear of rejection and embarrassment can become paralyzing barriers when it comes to building relationships with others. Often, these feelings create mental excuses that convince us it's not the "right time" to establish a relationship or contact. These self-imposed barriers can limit our networking opportunities and personal and professional growth. Overcoming this obstacle requires recognizing these internal excuses, challenging them, and reminding ourselves that every moment is an opportunity to connect and enrich our networks.

But I'll give you three keys that can help you overcome such a situation.

1. Change Your Mental Concept of the Event
The first key involves changing your perspective: instead of viewing these events as stressful, see them as exciting opportunities to meet and connect with fascinating people.

2. Practice Your Elevator Pitch

Facing new situations or challenges can be a source of anxiety and nervousness. However, practicing and perfecting your brief presentation speech, also known as the "elevator pitch," is a proven technique to mitigate these feelings. This exercise will provide you with more than just security; it will give you palpable confidence and help you effectively communicate who you are and what you offer in networking situations.

3. Set Realistic Goals

Instead of overwhelming yourself with impractical expectations, identify achievable and meaningful goals for the event. Setting realistic objectives will allow you to enjoy the networking process, focusing on quality connections rather than quantity. This will not only reduce the pressure you may feel but also give you a sense of accomplishment as you reach your specific goals for the event. Remember that each positive interaction contributes to the growth of your professional network.

Overcoming the Fear and Embarrassment of Networking

AUTHOR'S NOTES ...

When it comes to addressing the fear or embarrassment associated with networking, it's important to understand that these feelings are common and natural for many people. Networking can be an intimidating experience, especially for those who are introverted or lack self-confidence in social settings. However, overcoming these obstacles is essential for building strong relationships and making the most of the professional opportunities that networking can offer.

Adopting a positive mindset, preparing adequately, and remembering that everyone shares similar feelings can help you face these challenges with confidence and determination. Ultimately, networking is about building meaningful relationships that can drive personal and professional growth.

"Networking is not about being perfect, but about being authentic. Be yourself and let your passion and enthusiasm for what you do shine through every interaction."

Be Likeable!

Being likeable involves interacting in a way that generates sympathy, appreciation, and respect.

My advice:

1. Show genuine appreciation and interest in others.

2. Remember the person's name and mention it in conversation.

3. Be a good listener, encourage others to talk about themselves, and discuss what interests them.

4. Make the other person feel important

"Business is about relationships. Sometimes it's easy to forget that people do business with those they like."

- Show Genuine Appreciation
- Remember Your Interlocutor's Name
- Be a Good Listener
- Make Your Interlocutor Feel Important

AUTHOR'S NOTES...

According to Dale Carnegie, author of the bestseller "How to Win Friends and Influence People":

"The name of a person is, to that person, the sweetest sound in any language."

I'm sure you've experienced this, just like I have: forgetting the name of someone you just met. Right after the handshake, their name seems to vanish like smoke. To avoid these awkward moments and improve your social and professional relationships, here are three simple techniques from Carnegie that will help you remember names effectively:

Repeat the Name During the Introduction:
In that first meeting, make a conscious effort to repeat the person's name. For example, instead of just saying "Nice to meet you," say "Nice to meet you, Ana" or "Pleased to meet you, Ana." If you didn't hear the name clearly, ask, "Sorry, can you repeat your name?" This simple act of repetition helps to anchor the name in your memory from the start.

Use the Name During the Conversation
Integrate their name naturally into the conversation. For example, you might say, "Ana, what brought you to this event?" Using their name several times not only solidifies your memory but also creates a more personal connection. And don't forget to repeat the name when saying goodbye: "It was a pleasure meeting you, Ana."

Repeat the Name Silently
While the other person is talking, silently repeat their name in your mind. This method is especially useful at social events where you're introduced to several people at once; it helps to avoid confusion between similar names and strengthens short-term memory.

"Every interaction with a person is an opportunity to expand your network and enrich your professional and personal life."

Convince People!

Convincing people to accept an idea or make a specific decision isn't easy. In addition to using arguments and persuasive tactics, it helps to keep in mind that:

The best way to win an argument is to avoid it. It's a good option to use "yes..., but...." For example: "Yes, you are absolutely right, but I would do it this way...."

Avoid directly telling someone they are wrong. Instead, try to guide the conversation towards the correct answer in a respectful and constructive manner.

> Use the Phrase "Yes..., But..."
>
> Example:
> "Yes, I understand your point about reducing operational costs, but I believe we could achieve a greater impact by investing in technology that, although initially more expensive, will provide us with a more substantial return on investment in the long term."

And if it turns out that you are the one who is wrong, don't hesitate to admit it immediately.

Honesty and humility are always appreciated and help build a more open and productive dialogue.

Foster an environment where the other person feels comfortable to speak more and express their ideas. This can involve asking open-ended questions that invite reflection and dialogue. By doing so, you can help the person come to conclusions on their own, which can make them feel more committed and invested in the idea as if it were their own. This strategy can be very effective in promoting collaboration and commitment.

It is essential to adopt an empathetic perspective and try to understand things from the other person's point of view. This will not only allow you to better understand their needs and concerns but also help you communicate more effectively and build a stronger and more meaningful relationship.

Considering that, according to British writer Graham Greene:

"You will never convince a mouse that a black cat brings good luck."

… this can help you:

- The best way to win an argument is to avoid it.

- Never tell your counterpart they are wrong.

- Let the idea come from your counterpart.

- Put yourself in your counterpart's shoes.

7

Principal Key to Success in Networking

Personal Keys to Project Success

MAIN KEY TO SUCCESS IN NETWORKING?

But...

Despite all the advice and guidelines detailed in this book, it is crucial not to lose sight of the essentials.

We must never confuse the problem or make an incorrect diagnosis.

The main key to success in networking is... (solution on the next page)

YOU !

The Keys to Personal Success in Projects

Just like in any professional or personal project, in networking, the main key to success will always be YOU! Here are seven essential attitudes for anyone who wants to succeed in their projects.

1. Have Fun
My advice is that if you're not having fun doing what you do, quit! Having fun is healthy. It's not an activity; it's a feeling that doesn't need to be scheduled. You don't have to have fun only during leisure moments.

2. Take Action
Things don't happen on their own. If you want to achieve something, YOU are the one who has to take action. There's a saying that goes, "Don't be afraid of going slow; be afraid of standing still." I recommend reading my book: "Objective: Dance!" 😉

3. Put Passion into Everything You Do
In everything you do, add that special ingredient called Passion.

4. Believe in Yourself

On the path to personal and professional success, the first obstacle many face is self-doubt. An old saying reminds us: "There will always be someone who doesn't believe in you; make sure it's not you." This maxim encapsulates a fundamental truth in personal and professional development: self-confidence is key.

5. Educate Yourself

"Success = Opportunity + Preparation." This equation, though simple in structure, holds a depth that has been explored by countless authors over time. The formula suggests a fundamental truth: to achieve success, it is not enough to be in the right place at the right time. Opportunity must find us well-prepared.

Preparation is a continuous process, a constant commitment to learning and personal growth. In today's fast-paced and technologically advanced world, education is not just a competitive advantage but a vital necessity.

6. Create Your Own Options

In the complexity of life, having options is more than a luxury; it is an essential need for self-determination and personal freedom. "If you have options, you decide; if you don't, others decide for you." This statement captures a fundamental principle: control over our lives comes from the options we can create and the decisions we can make. Networking is a key tool for creating options.

7. Create Value, Meet Needs, and Differentiate from the Competition

Always remember that the heart of any successful business, whether it offers a product, a service, or an activity, lies in its ability to provide significant value and meet real needs in society. If what you propose does not meet these essential criteria, its sustainability and future are seriously compromised.

Besides creating value and meeting needs, it is vital to differentiate yourself from the competition. In a saturated market, standing out can be as crucial as offering a good product or service.

AUTHOR'S NOTES ...

Having Fun Helps Build Relationships

When we find ourselves in a joyful and fun state, our body reacts in surprising and profoundly beneficial ways. One of these reactions is the secretion of a "hard drug," dopamine, a neurotransmitter popularly known as the "molecule of happiness." This chemical not only makes us feel good but also enhances our ability to face challenges and adverse situations more effectively.

Dopamine increases our concentration, improves our decision-making ability, and boosts our motivation. Being in a heightened dopamine state allows us to tackle complex problems with a more creative and less fearful perspective. Indeed, this favorable chemical state transforms our mental approach, leading us to see difficulties not as insurmountable obstacles but as opportunities to learn and grow.

Moreover, dopamine plays a crucial role in regulating our mood and emotions, helping us maintain a positive attitude in the face of challenges.

This neurotransmitter also facilitates social connection, which is essential for building supportive relationships that can be crucial during difficult times.

Therefore, cultivating moments of joy and fun is not only vital for our emotional well-being but also essential for our effectiveness at work and in daily life. It makes us more resilient and adaptable, capable of handling the unpredictable waves of everyday life with grace and efficiency.

Author's Video on Personal Success Keys

Personal Keys to Success in Projects

- Have Fun!
- Move!
- Put Passion into It
- Believe in Yourself
- Educate Yourself
- Create Your Options
- Add Value, Fulfill a Need, Stand Out

8
WCONNECTA

WCONNECTA

In 2010, as the head of the Wtransnet Foundation, now known as the Mereze Foundation, I embarked on an exciting project: the creation of WCONNECTA, the most prominent networking event in the logistics and transportation sector in Europe.

This event continues to be a notable celebration today, solidifying itself as an essential space for interaction and collaboration in the transport and logistics sector. Each year, it becomes a key date in the agendas of major European companies.

The format of the event was designed with the goal of promoting and facilitating contact between professionals in the sector. Upon registering, each professional completed a form detailing their professional DNA, that is, their needs and services offered.
This enabled the creation of personalized agendas, freeing attendees from worries by indicating the relevant place and time where they needed to go.

The event featured three main areas for participant interactions, each favoring a specific type of meeting.

The first area, known as "Speed Networking," brought professionals together at long tables to connect with others offering the services they needed or were looking for. These sessions consisted of 7-minute interviews during blocks of approximately 1 hour.

The second space, the "Cargo Area," provided major European logistics companies with a personalized space to conduct pre-scheduled interviews with European transport companies through the event's platform.

The third zone, the "Coffee Area," offered a café-like environment to foster relationships between professionals who happened to meet unexpectedly at the event. These encounters took place in a relaxed setting while enjoying a coffee.

The success of this event, partly attributed to its format, lies in addressing a common issue in such events: the "fear" and "embarrassment" people often experience when approaching or contacting others. This obstacle was overcome using "ice breaker" techniques. These included providing a clear agenda that facilitated professional interactions and a personalized "business assistant" service.

Attending professionals didn't have to worry about anything, as the organization took care of absolutely everything for them.

*"Ice breakers" are activities or exercises designed to ease tension, create a more pleasant atmosphere, and facilitate interaction among participants in meetings, conferences, workshops, or any group event. Their main purpose is to help people feel more comfortable, promote communication, and foster a collaborative environment.

Video 9th Edition of the Wconnecta Event Madrid 2018

9
NETWORKING IN ACTION

NETWORKING IN ACTION

Networking in Action - A Vision for the Future

As you turn the last pages of the book, one thing becomes clear: the art of networking is much more than a skill; it is a philosophy of life that, when practiced with passion and purpose, can open up a universe of opportunities.

The true power of what you have learned lies not only in the concepts and techniques but in how these tools can unlock unexpected opportunities and enrich your professional life. Imagine a near future where every social or professional event you attend, every meeting you participate in, not only expands your network but also deepens the connections you already have. Think of how every conversation is a seed that, with proper care, can bloom into a fruitful collaboration, a trusted mentor, or a path to new horizons.

But in this final chapter, I invite you not only to reflect on what you've learned; I challenge you to act!

Networking in action

Start by identifying a networking opportunity this week, whether it's a virtual coffee with a colleague you haven't seen in a while or attending an industry event where you can network with other professionals. Use the strategies from this guide to establish a genuine connection. Notice how even a small gesture of authenticity and curiosity can completely transform an ordinary professional relationship into an extraordinary one.

Finally, as you close this book, remember that every end is simply the beginning of something new. Let this not be the end of your learning but the launch of your journey towards mastering networking. You are equipped with the knowledge, tools, and inspiration to change not only your own life but also the lives of those around you.

Act, connect, transform. The world of networking awaits you.

I sincerely hope this book has enriched your perspective and provided you with valuable tools.

If you wish to discuss any idea, express your comments, or simply share your reflections on the topics covered, I encourage you to contact me. You can email me at jmsalles@josemariasalles.com.

I would be delighted to receive your messages and hear your thoughts. Thank you for sharing this learning journey with me, and I look forward to hearing from you soon!

www.ingramcontent.com/pod-product-compliance
Lightning Source LLC
Chambersburg PA
CBHW071930210526
45479CB00002B/618